TABLE OF CONTENTS

Unless otherwise indicated, all Scripture quotations are taken from the King James Version of the Bible.
Battle Techniques For War Weary Saints
ISBN 10: 1-56394-023-X / ISBN 13: 978-1563940231 / B-07
Copyright © 2001 by **MIKE MURDOCK**
All publishing rights belong exclusively to Wisdom International
Publisher/Editor: Deborah Murdock Johnson
Published by The Wisdom Center · 4051 Denton Hwy. · Ft. Worth, Texas 76117
1-817-759-2665 · 1-817-759-BOOK · 1-817-759-0300
You Will Love Our Website..! V

Struggle Is Merely
The Proof
You Have Not Yet
Been Conquered.

-MIKE MURDOCK

❧ 1 ❧

YOUR HEAVENLY FATHER IS CONCERNED ABOUT YOUR BATTLES IN LIFE

Your Battles Matter To God.

God has called and anointed me to help you achieve your dreams and goals for your life. What is your *biggest* dream today? Do your obstacles appear insurmountable? Are you in the struggle of your life-time? Then, get your faith up! Though battle is not always your choice...*winning is.*

That is why your faith in God is so important.

You are already a winner. The fact that you are reading this book is proof of your willingness to learn. *The teachable are reachable.*

My own life has been a parade of such battles and triumphs—seasons of struggle that have produced incredible miracles. I have learned that *Struggle Is Merely The Proof That You Have Not Yet Been Conquered.*

"When thou passest through the waters, I will be with thee; and through the rivers, they shall not overflow thee: when thou walkest through the fire, thou shalt not be burned; neither shall the flame kindle upon thee," (Isaiah 43:2).

God anticipated your pain. That is why there was a cross. Though your failures are planned by hell, your recovery is far more organized by Heaven!

"Though I walk in the midst of trouble, Thou wilt revive me:...The Lord will perfect that which concerneth me," (Psalm 138:7-8).

What Is Battle?

What do I mean by the battles or struggles in your life? Any opposition, pain or difficulty that you encounter while attempting to obey an instruction from God...or complete His dreams in your life...or to receive a desired miracle He has planned.

Your battle is any pain produced during your efforts to satisfy God's expectations of you.

For example, Daniel's desire to please the Lord in his prayer life activated enemies that resulted in his Lions' Den Experience.

2

YOU WILL ALWAYS HAVE AN ENEMY

You Were Born Into An Adversarial Environment.
Your Enemy is lucifer, not flesh and blood. People
are simply *channels and tools* for your Enemy. Paul
wrote, "For we wrestle not against flesh and blood, but
against principalities, against powers, against rulers of
the darkness of this world, against spiritual wickedness in
high places," (Ephesians 6:12).

Your real Enemy is the devil...satan... lucifer. "Be sober,
be vigilant; because your adversary the devil, as a roaring
lion, walketh about, seeking whom he may devour," (1 Peter
5:8).

Who is he? An ex-employee of Heaven. *He is a fallen
angel.* "...I beheld satan as lightening fall from Heaven,"
(Luke 10:18). *Your adversary's time is limited.* So, his
efforts are intense. "...for the devil is come down unto you,
having great wrath, because he knoweth that he hath but
a short time," (Revelation 12:12).

Your Enemy's power to tempt you is limited. "...but
God is faithful, Who will not suffer you to be tempted
above that ye are able; but will with the temptation
also make a way to escape, that ye may be able to bear
it," (1 Corinthians 10:13).

Let's Review!

▶ Anything Good Is Hated By Everything Evil.
▶ You Can Discern Evil By Its Reaction To Truth And Those Who Teach It.
▶ Your Enemy Is Satan And Those Willing To Become His Instrument of Pain To Others.
▶ Your Enemy Is Limited And Cannot Control You Nor The Assignment God Has Birthed Within You.

3

YOUR ENEMY IS DECEPTIVE

Satan Is A Liar.

Satan despises God and he hates anything that receives God's affection. He is quite aware of God's unusual care and protection of us and reacts with unbridled resentment. His reaction to the blessings upon Job is a prime example:

"Hast not Thou made an hedge about him, and about his house, and about all that he hath on every side? Thou hast blessed the work of his hands, and his substance is increased in the land," (Job 1:10).

Satan is deceptive, cunning, manipulative and the father of all lies. "Ye are of your father the devil, and the lusts of your father ye will do. He was a murderer from the beginning, and abode not in the truth, because there is no truth in him. When he speaketh a lie, he speaketh of his own: for he is a liar, and the father of it," (John 8:44).

Satan Resents
Anything God Loves.

-MIKE MURDOCK

4

SATAN IS ENVIOUS OF THE AFFECTION GOD HAS TOWARD YOU

Satan Was Jealous of Job.

He opposes you because you are a potential *Source* of pleasure to God. "...for Thou hast created all things, and for Thy pleasure they are and were created," (Revelation 4:11).

Satan's real enemy is God. But because he is powerless against God, he attacks that which is closest to the heart of God...you and me.

Satan's main purpose of warfare is to pain God's heart. To insult Him...to frustrate His purposes in your life. He wants you to grieve God's heart by doubting His integrity.

"God is not a man, that He should lie; neither the son of man, that He should repent: hath He said, and shall He not do it? or hath He spoken, and shall He not make it good?" (Numbers 23:19).

Satan wants to abort the arrival of any miracle that would bring glory to God. He wants to paralyze your planning...abort your dreams...dilute your hope.

Broken Focus
     Is The Only Reason
Men Fail.

-MIKE MURDOCK

∼ 5 ∼

YOU CAN DISCERN SATAN'S FAVORITE WEAPONS

4 Common Weapons

1.   **Delays**—When satan tries to thwart the arrival of a desired miracle. He knows that a *delay* can weaken your desire to keep reaching.

Daniel shares this kind of experience in Daniel 10:2-14.

2.   **Deceit**—Satan is a master at deception and error. He knows that if he can infiltrate a generation through erroneous teaching, he can destroy millions. One single falsehood from the mouth of a clever reporter can damage the faith of millions.

Only eternity will reveal how many dreams have crashed on the rocks of prejudiced teachings against Divine healing...or The Holy Spirit...or financial prosperity.

3.   **Distractions**—*Broken focus is the goal of all satanic attacks.* "Turn not to the right hand nor to the left," (Proverbs 4:27). Your energy and time is too precious to waste on unproductive friendships, unworthy criticisms or other distracting interests.

After a newspaper attack on my ministry, my attorneys and CPAs phoned me. They were so angry.

"We found 36 false statements in the first news article alone! Do you want to sue?"

I laughed. "Of course not. I have an Assignment

from God. Billy Graham explained well why he did not respond to all his critics when he said that his enemies would not believe his explanation; his friends did not require it. God is our defense."

   4.   **Disappointment**—With yourself or others. Do not replay the guilt of previous mistakes, nor become preoccupied with past losses, nor magnify the weaknesses of others. Remember, *satan's favorite entry point will always be through those closest to your heart.*

closest to my heart

Jennifer
Taylor,
Travis

⚬ 6 ⚬

YOU CAN PREDICT SEASONS OF SATANIC ATTACK

Satan Is Not Omnipresent.

He cannot be everywhere at the same time. He attacks in *seasons.*

There are 6 specific seasons when you may personally experience unusual spiritual warfare in your life.

    1. When You Become Physically Exhausted. I travel a lot. Sometimes, up to 20,000 miles in a single month. I have noticed that my faith and enthusiasm wane through fatigue. In fact, satan's greatest attacks on your faith life will probably happen when you get little or no sleep.

    2. When You Face Major Decisions In Your Life. This may be in your career or even geographic relocation. That is why patience is so beneficial. "The Lord is good unto them that wait for Him," (Lamentations 3:25).

    3. The Birth of A Child Destined To Become A Spiritual Leader. It happened after the birth of Moses when Pharaoh commanded the male children to be murdered.

"And he said, When ye do the office of a midwife to the Hebrew women, and see them upon the stools; if it be a son, then ye shall kill him: but if it be a daughter, then she shall live," (Exodus 1:16). Also, the birth of

Jesus. "...for Herod will seek the young child to destroy Him," (Matthew 2:13). Great people often relate childhood adversities that threatened them in their early life.

4. When A Specific Miracle Has Just Left The Hand of God Toward You. Daniel waited 21 days for his prayer to be answered. When the angel of the Lord finally appeared, he explained the warfare that necessitated the assistance of Michael, the archangel to help him. "But the prince of the kingdom of Persia withstood me one and twenty days: but, lo, Michael, one of the chief princes, came to help me; and I remained there with the kings of Persia," (Daniel 10:13). So you see, your battle is really a signal that something is en route to you from God today.

5. When You Launch A New Ministry For God. Jesus faced His wilderness experience just prior to His healing ministry (read Matthew 4). I have seen it happen, almost without fail, every major project, new television effort or new church building program encounters extreme opposition or setbacks.

The timing of my attacks was interesting. Actually, the reporters first sat in my ministry four years before they finally released their articles. The timing reveals so much! The articles came just *after* I began...

▶ A national television outreach on a major secular TV network.
▶ Feeding and supporting 1,000 children a day to be fed daily in Mexico.
▶ Sponsoring the *Mike Murdock Home of Hope,* a boys' orphanage for children afflicted with AIDS in South Africa.

6.   When You Are Next In Line For A Promotion From God. When Joseph announced the dream that God had given him, his own brothers, in bitterness, sold him into slavery. His reputation of honor was stripped because of one lie from Potiphar's wife. Yet, each day of adversity simply ushered him one day closer to the throne.

▶ Every Season Has A Different Product.

▶ Warfare Is A Clue That Satan Anticipates Your Promotion.

▶ Pace Yourself For The Journey.
"And let us not be weary in well doing: for in due season we shall reap, if we faint not," (Galatians 6:9).

The Word of God
Becomes
The Energy of God
Within You.

-MIKE MURDOCK

7

YOU MUST USE YOUR 6 MOST EFFECTIVE WEAPONS

You Will <u>Never Win A *Spiritual* Battle Logically.</u> "For the weapons of our warfare are not carnal, but mighty through God to the pulling down of strong holds," (2 Corinthians 10:4).

You will never win a spiritual battle through your own strength or Wisdom. "Not by might, nor by power, but by my spirit, saith the Lord of hosts," (Zechariah 4:6).

1. You Must Know And Speak The Word of God. "For the Word of God is quick, and powerful, and sharper than any two-edged sword, piercing even to the dividing asunder of soul and spirit, and of the joints and marrow, and is a discerner of the thoughts and intents of the heart," (Hebrews 4:12).

2. Your Conversations Should Reflect The Mentality of A Conqueror. "Death and life are in the power of the tongue: and they that love it shall eat the fruit thereof," (Proverbs 18:21).

3. You Must Take Your Authority Over Satan In The Name of Jesus. "The name of the Lord is a strong tower: the righteous runneth into it, and is safe," (Proverbs 18:10). "Wherefore God also hath highly exalted him, and given him a name which is above every name: That at the name of Jesus every knee should bow, of things in Heaven, and things in earth, and things under the earth," (Philippians 2:9-10).

4. You Must In Faith, Clothe Yourself In Spiritual Armor Each Morning In Prayer. "Wherefore take unto you the whole armor of God, that ye may be able to withstand in the evil day, and having done all, to stand," (Ephesians 6:13).

5. You Must Respect The Power of Prayer And Fasting. "The effectual fervent prayer of a righteous man availeth much," (James 5:16). "Is not this the fast that I have chosen? to loose the bands of wickedness, to undo the heavy burdens, and to let the oppressed go free, and that ye break every yoke?" (Isaiah 58:6).

6. You Must Pursue And Extract The Wisdom of God From The Spiritual Mentors He Places In Your Life. "A wise man will hear, and will increase learning; and a man of understanding shall attain unto wise counsels," (Proverbs 1:5).

The newspaper reporters were almost ruthless and disturbing in their insistence on a personal interview. I even spent 25 minutes with the major reporter and even prayed for him inside The Wisdom Center. But, he was incredibly disrespectful in the pursuit of a personal interview. So, I talked to a major mentor of mine. He is a 70 year old pastor with over 50 years of experience with the media and has 200 churches under his authority. He spoke to me some remarkable counsel:

"Mike, I have spent over 50 years working with media and trying to give them what they wanted. In over 50 years of ministry, I have yet for one single report to use the documents we provided and speak favorably. They are not pursuing truth. They want to destroy and stain the reputation of proven men of God whose truth has provoked them to anger. They will write the story they want to write...with your help or without your help."

I replied, "They want me to give them an interview, but they are refusing to print my answers with the questions they ask."

"Do not provide them an interview. They are disqualified for your access and your time because of their disrespect and evil motives."

▶ Nobody Else Can Fight Your Battle For You.
▶ Nobody Else Can Feel Your Pain.
▶ Nobody Can Make The Decisions You Must Make.

RECOMMENDED INVESTMENT:
Wisdom For Crisis Times (Book/B-40/112 pg)

The Seasons of Your Life
Will Change
Every Time You Decide
To Use Your Faith.

-MIKE MURDOCK

❧ 8 ❧

DISCERN THE 4 FORCES THAT SHORTEN YOUR SEASONS OF STRUGGLE

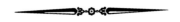

Seasons That Begin...Can End.

4 Forces Must Be Discerned

1.   Your Speaking...words of faith that build you up in the Spirit. Faith talk is explosive. "Death and life are in the power of the tongue: and they that love it shall eat the fruit thereof," (Proverbs 18:21)

2.   Your Singing...creates a climate satan cannot tolerate. Songs of worship and praise *dispel* demonic spirits as Saul discovered when David played. "And it came to pass, when the evil spirit from God was upon Saul, that David took an harp, and played with his hand: so Saul was refreshed, and was well, and the evil spirit departed from him," (1 Samuel 16:23).

News reporters wrote sneering and mocking words about my singing to The Holy Spirit. They contemptuously said they were love songs to women and belittled such emphasis on The Holy Spirit. You see, satan despises your love songs to The Holy Spirit...so learn and develop this weapon.

3.   Your Sharing...in prayer of agreement with others. It is wise for you to initiate the prayer assistance of intercessors. "Verily I say unto you, Whatsoever ye shall bind on earth shall be bound in Heaven: and whatsoever ye shall loose on earth shall be loosed in Heaven. Again I say unto you, That if two of you shall agree on earth as touching any thing that they shall ask, it shall be done for them of My Father which is in Heaven," (Matthew 18:18-19).

4.   Your Seed-Sowing...creates a partnership with God that involves Him in your adversity. "Bring ye all the tithes into the storehouse, that there may be meat in Mine house, and prove Me now herewith, saith the Lord of hosts, if I will not open you the windows of Heaven, and pour you out a blessing, that there shall not be room enough to receive it. And I will rebuke the devourer for your sakes, and he shall not destroy the fruits of your ground; neither shall your vine cast her fruit before the time in the field, saith the Lord of hosts," (Malachi 3:10-11).

I have always observed significant changes in times of stress, battle and struggle when I have boldly unleashed these 4 forces.

RECOMMENDED INVESTMENT:
How To Walk Through Fire And Not Be Burned (CD/CDS-03)

⬲ 9 ⬲

20 WISDOM KEYS AND TECHNIQUES TO REMEMBER DURING AN UNCOMMON BATTLE

1. **You Will Never Outgrow Warfare, You Simply Must Learn To Fight.** "For we wrestle not against flesh and blood, but against principalities, against powers, against the rulers of the darkness of this world, against spiritual wickedness in high places," (Ephesians 6:12).

2. **God's Purpose In Your Crisis Is Not Your Survival, But Your Education.** "All the commandments which I command thee this day shall ye observe to do, that ye may live, and multiply, and go in and possess the land which the Lord sware unto your fathers. And thou shalt remember all the way which the Lord thy God led thee these forty years in the wilderness, to humble thee, and to prove thee, to know what was in thine heart, whether thou wouldest keep His commandments, or no," (Deuteronomy 8:1-2).

3. **Nothing Is Ever As Bad As It First Appears.** "Though I walk in the midst of trouble, Thou wilt revive me: Thou shalt stretch forth Thine hand against the wrath of mine enemies, and Thy right hand shall save me. The Lord will perfect that which concerneth me: Thy mercy, O Lord, endureth for ever: forsake not the works of Thine own hands," (Psalm 138:7-8).

Attacks on you will stir up the loyalty of true friends who have discerned your integrity and truthfulness. Attack is a purging time that eliminates those who are unqualified to participate in your life and vision.

4. Failure Is Not An Event, But An Opinion. "And the people stood beholding. And the rulers also with them derided Him, saying, He saved others; let Him save Himself, if He be Christ, the chosen of God," (Luke 23:35).

When your enemy attacks you, examine His opinion and views of the other things you love.

When I talked to the reporter at The Wisdom Center, I wanted to know his views on those things that I valued.

He was contemptuous and scornful of the healing ministry of our day saying that people just "*think* they are healed."

Why was Stephen stoned? He was stoned by the very people who despised the Jesus within him.

The anointing of The Holy Spirit within him, agitated those who despise the holiness of a pure God.

5. Failure Cannot Happen In Your Life Without Your Permission. "And if it seem evil unto you to serve the Lord, choose you this day whom ye will serve; whether the gods which your fathers served that were on the other side of the flood, or the gods of the Amorites, in whose land ye dwell: but as for me and my house, we will serve the Lord," (Joshua 24:15).

6. All Great Men Attract Satanic Attention. "Then satan answered the Lord, and said, Doth Job fear God for nought? Hast not Thou made an hedge about him, and about his house, and about all that he hath on every side? Thou hast blessed the work of his hands, and his substance is increased in the land. But put forth Thine hand now, and touch all that he hath, and he will curse Thee to Thy face. And the Lord said unto satan, Behold, all that he hath is in thy power; only upon himself put not forth thine hand. So satan went forth from the presence of the Lord," (Job 1:9-12).

Your adversity is always proportionate to your eventual and potential influence.

Men whose voice is feared in hell...will always become the focus of satanic attack.

7. All Men Fall...The Great Ones Get Back Up. "The steps of a good man are ordered by the Lord: and he delighteth in His way. Though he fall, he shall not be utterly cast down: for the Lord upholdeth him with His hand," (Psalm 37:23-24).

8. Satan Always Attacks What He Fears The Most. "When Herod the king had heard these things, he was troubled, and all Jerusalem with him," (Matthew 2:3).

9. Struggle Is The Proof You Have Not Yet Been Conquered. "We are troubled on every side, yet not distressed; we are perplexed, but not in despair; Persecuted, but not forsaken; cast down, but not destroyed," (2 Corinthians 4:8-9).

Why are we attacked? You have not yet lost. Satan believes in you also. He fears what you can accomplish. If satan believes that you can achieve your goal...why shouldn't you believe you can achieve that goal?

10. Satan's Favorite Entry Point Will Always Be Through Those Closest To You. "For the son dishonoureth the father, the daughter riseth up against her mother, the daughter in law against her mother in law; a man's enemies are the men of his own house," (Micah 7:6).

After 3 days of bombardment and an effort to destroy the credibility of our ministry, a major Christian magazine in the southern part of the United States called me. It is a magazine known around the world. The editors indicated that they wanted to present my side in response to the newspaper article. In fact, I even prayed with them over the phone as they assured me, "We will print every word you say." Hours later, their article was shockingly destructive as ninety percent of the article were the quotations of the sadistic and destructive people who had written the newspaper articles. They left out over 50 percent of my statement and misused the answers that I had given.

I could hardly believe what I saw. I had taken them into my confidence...believing in their sincerity. After all, these were supposedly Christians who were trying to promote the work of the Lord. I saw them immediately as the Trojan horse of Christianity... brought inside the camp of Christianity to bring destruction to those in the ministry.

What someone will do to another...they will eventually do to you.

11. You Will Never Win A Spiritual Battle Logically. "For though we walk in the flesh, we do not war after the flesh," (2 Corinthians 10:3).

Never use the weapons your enemy has chosen. David understood this powerful principal. He complained to Saul that he could not use his armor. He stayed with the weapon that he had proven every single day of his life.

12. Pain Is Merely A Passage To A Miracle.
"For His anger endureth but a moment; in His favour is life: weeping may endure for a night, but joy cometh in the morning," (Psalm 30:5).

13. Warfare Always Surrounds The Birth of A Miracle. "And when they were departed, behold, the angel of the Lord appeareth to Joseph in a dream, saying, Arise, and take the young child and His mother, and flee into Egypt, and be thou there until I bring thee word: for Herod will seek the young child to destroy Him," (Matthew 2:13).

14. Crisis Always Occurs At The Curve of Change. "And Abram went up out of Egypt, he, and his wife, and all that he had, and Lot with him, into the south. And the land was not able to bear them, that they might dwell together: for their substance was great, so that they could not dwell together. And there was a strife between the herdmen of Abram's cattle and the herdmen of Lot's cattle: and the Canaanite and the Perizzite dwelled then in the land," (Genesis 13:1,6-7).

15. Satan Always Attacks Those Who Are Next In Line For A Promotion. "And the Lord said unto satan, hast thou considered My servant Job, that there is none like him in the earth, a perfect and an upright man, one that feareth God, and escheweth evil? and still he holdeth fast his integrity, although thou movedst Me against him, to destroy him without cause," (Job 2:3).

16. Stop Looking At What You Can See And Start Looking At What You Can Have. "If the Lord delight in us, then He will bring us into this land, and give it us; a land which floweth with milk and honey," (Numbers 14:8).

17. No One Has Been A Loser Longer Than Satan. "And the great dragon was cast out, that old serpent, called the devil, and satan, which deceiveth the whole world: he was cast out into the earth, and his angels were cast out with him," (Revelation 12:9).

18. Never Speak Words That Make Satan Think He Is Winning. "If it be so, our God Whom we serve is able to deliver us from the burning fiery furnace, and He will deliver us out of thine hand, O king," (Daniel 3:17).

19. Those Unwilling To Lose, Rarely Do. "Cast thy burden upon the Lord, and He shall sustain thee: He shall never suffer the righteous to be moved," (Psalm 55:22).

20. Battle Is Your Chance For Recognition... Both In Heaven And Hell. "Fight the good fight of faith, lay hold on eternal life, whereunto thou art also called, and hast professed a good profession before many witnesses," (1 Timothy 6:12).

God is only authorized to promote an overcomer (see Revelation 2,3).

SPECIAL MEMO TO SPIRITUAL SOLDIERS

Accurately Access Your Struggle. Name your real enemy for who he is.

Make a quality decision to stay focused. You have already been in your past. There was nothing there that you wanted, so fight it out to get into your future. *Do battle.* Your *endurance* is demoralizing to satan. The *rewards* of overcoming are worth a thousand times more than any pain you will ever experience.

The Size of Your Enemy Determines The Size of Your Reward. So, get excited! Your future is close. Your promotion is inevitable.

31 WISDOM KEYS

1. Never Complain About What You Permit.
2. Crisis Always Occurs At The Curve of Change.
3. Your Enemy Is Not A Wall, But A Door To Your Next Season.
4. When You Ask God For A Future, He Will Schedule An Adversary.
5. Anything Good Is Hated By Everything Evil.
6. The Problem That Infuriates You The Most Is The Problem You Have Been Assigned To Solve.
7. The Size of Your Enemy Determines The Size of Your Reward.
8. Your Reaction To A Man of God Determines God's Reaction To You.
9. Struggle Is The Proof You Have Not Yet Been Conquered.
10. Crisis Will Purge Every Relationship Unwilling To Discern Your Integrity.
11. What You Can Tolerate You Cannot Change.
12. Attack Is The Proof Your Enemy Anticipates Your Success.
13. Satan Attacks Anything God Has Chosen To Promote.
14. What You Fail To Destroy Will Eventually Destroy You.
15. False Accusation Is The Last Stage Before Supernatural Promotion.

16. Warfare Always Surrounds The Birth of A Miracle.
17. You Cannot Outgrow Warfare, You Must Simply Learn To Fight.
18. What God Loves Satan Hates.
19. Anger Is Simply Passion Requiring An Appropriate Focus.
20. You Cannot Conquer What You Refuse To Hate.
21. Battle Is The Stage Where Loyalty Is Proven.
22. Never Enter A Battle That Does Not Offer A Reward.
23. Silence Cannot Be Misquoted.
24. Never Spend More Time On An Enemy Than You Would Give To A Friend.
25. The Seasons of Your Life Will Change Every Time You Decide To Use Your Faith.
26. Never Speak Words That Make An Enemy Think He Is Winning.
27. Friends Create Comfort; Enemies Create Reward.
28. Overcoming Is The Authorization For God To Promote You.
29. Someone's Future Depends On Your Overcoming.
30. The Purpose of Your Memory Is To Replay Past Victories.
31. You Will Only Be Remembered For The Enemy You Overcome or The Enemy That Overcame You.

DECISION

Will You Accept Jesus As Your Personal Savior Today?

The Bible says, "That if thou shalt confess with thy mouth the Lord Jesus, and shalt believe in thine heart that God hath raised Him from the dead, thou shalt be saved" (Romans 10:9).

Pray this prayer from your heart today!

"Dear Jesus, I believe that You died for me and rose again on the third day. I confess I am a sinner...I need Your love and forgiveness...Come into my heart. Forgive my sins. I receive Your eternal life. Confirm Your love by giving me peace, joy and supernatural love for others. Amen."

DR. MIKE MURDOCK

is in tremendous demand as one of the most dynamic speakers in America today.

More than 17,000 audiences in over 100 countries have attended his Schools of Wisdom and conferences. Hundreds of invitations come to him from churches, colleges and business corporations. He is a noted author of over 250 books, including the best sellers, *The Leadership Secrets of Jesus* and *Secrets of the Richest Man Who Ever Lived.* Thousands view his weekly television program, *Wisdom Keys with Mike Murdock.* Many attend his Schools of Wisdom that he hosts in many cities of America.

Clip and Mail

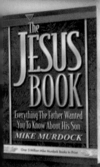

Crisis 7 BOOK PAK!

❶ The Survival Bible (Book/B-29/248pg/$12)

❷ Wisdom For Crisis Times (Book/B-40/112pg/$9)

❸ Seeds of Wisdom on Motivating Yourself (Book/B-171/32pg/$5)

❹ Seeds of Wisdom on Overcoming (Book/B-17/32pg/$5)

❺ Seeds of Wisdom on Warfare (Book/B-19/32pg/$5)

❻ Battle Techniques For War Weary Saints (Book/B-07/32pg/$5)

❼ Seeds of Wisdom on Adversity (Book/B-21/32pg/$5)

Each Wisdom Book may be purchased separately if so desired.

B THE WISDOM CENTER
4051 Denton Highway • Fort Worth, TX 76117

1-817-759-BOOK
1-817-759-2665
1-817-759-0300

You Will Love Our Website..!
MIKEMURDOCKBOOKS.COM

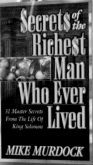

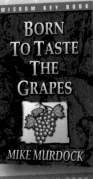

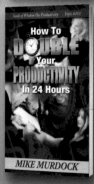

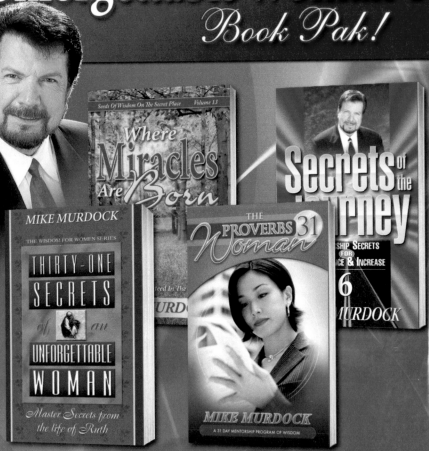

Millionaire-Talk

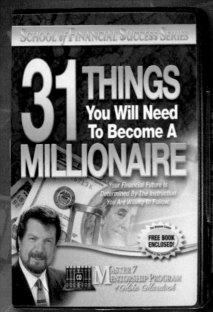

SCHOOL of FINANCIAL SUCCESS SERIES

31 THINGS You Will Need To Become A MILLIONAIRE

Your Financial Future Is Determined By The Instruction You Are Willing To Follow.

FREE BOOK ENCLOSED!

MASTER 7 MENTORSHIP PROGRAM of Mike Murdock

DR. MIKE MURDOCK

MY GIFT OF APPRECIATION
GIFT of Appreciation
Wisdom Is The Principal Thing

31 Things You Will Need To Become A Millionaire (2-CD's/SOWL-116)

Topics Include:

- You Will Need Financial Heroes
- Your Willingness To Negotiate Everything
- You Must Have The Ability To Transfer Your Enthusiasm, Your Vision To Others
- Know Your Competition
- Be Willing To Train Your Team Personally As To Your Expectations
- Hire Professionals To Do A Professional's Job

I have asked the Lord for 3,000 special partners who will sow an extra Seed of $58 towards our Television Outreach Ministry. Your Seed is so appreciated! Remember to request your Gift CD's, 2 Disc Volume, 31 Things You Will Need To Become A Millionaire, when you write this week!

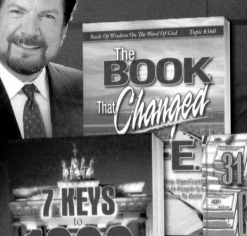
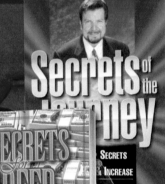
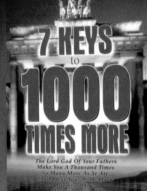

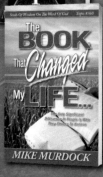

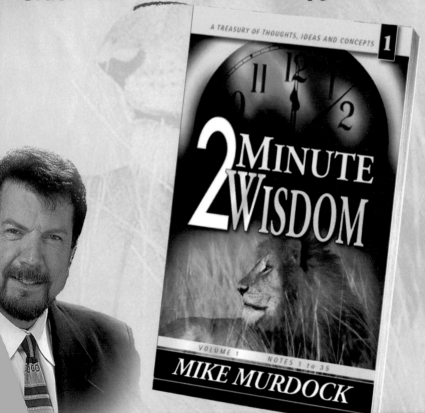

THE WISDOM BIBLE

Partnership Edition

Over 120 Wisdom Study Guides Included Such As:

▸ 10 Qualities of Uncommon Achievers
▸ 18 Facts You Should Know About The Anointing
▸ 21 Facts To Help You Identify Those Assigned To You
▸ 31 Facts You Should Know About Your Assignment
▸ 8 Keys That Unlock Victory In Every Attack
▸ 22 Defense Techniques To Remember During Seasons of Personal Attack
▸ 20 Wisdom Keys And Techniques To Remember During An Uncommon Battle
▸ 11 Benefits You Can Expect From God
▸ 31 Facts You Should Know About Favor
▸ The Covenant of 58 Blessings
▸ 7 Keys To Receiving Your Miracle
▸ 16 Facts You Should Remember About Contentious People
▸ 5 Facts Solomon Taught About Contracts
▸ 7 Facts You Should Know About Conflict
▸ 6 Steps That Can Unlock Your Self-Confidence
▸ And Much More!

Your Partnership makes such a difference in The Wisdom Center Outreach Ministries. I wanted to place a Gift in your hand that could last a lifetime for you and your family...**The Wisdom Study Bible.**

40 Years of Personal Notes...this Partnership Edition Bible contains 160 pages of my Personal Study Notes...that could forever change your Bible Study of The Word of God. This **Partnership Edition...**is my personal **Gift of Appreciation** when you sow your Sponsorship Seed of $1,000 for our Television Outreach Ministry. An Uncommon Seed Always Creates An Uncommon Harvest!

Mike

Thank you from my heart for your Seed of Obedience (Luke 6:38).

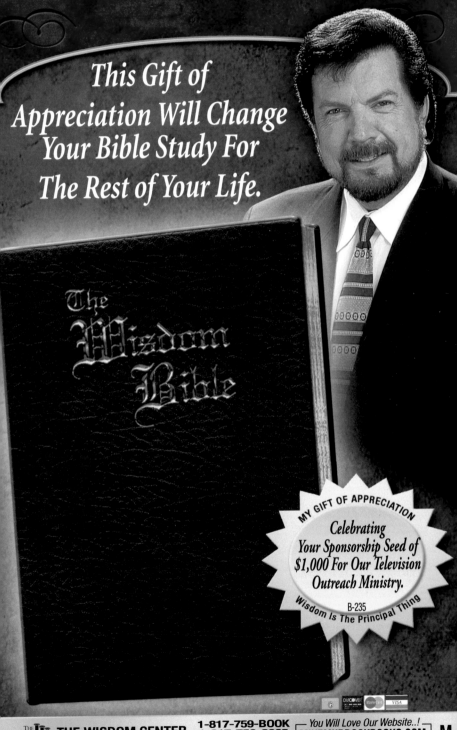

This Gift of Appreciation Will Change Your Bible Study For The Rest of Your Life.

The Wisdom Bible

MY GIFT OF APPRECIATION
Celebrating Your Sponsorship Seed of $1,000 For Our Television Outreach Ministry.
B-235
Wisdom Is The Principal Thing

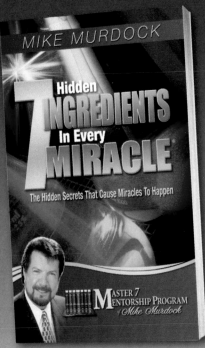